Stan Musial

Baseball Hero

James N. Giglio

Truman State University Press
Kirksville, Missouri

Notable Missourians

Cover art: Stan Musial, 1942, courtesy National Baseball Hall of Fame and Museum.

Cover design: Teresa Wheeler

Library of Congress Cataloging-in-Publication Data

Giglio, James N., 1939-
    Stan Musial : baseball hero / James Giglio.
              pages cm. — (Notable Missourians)
    Includes bibliographical references and index.
    ISBN 978-1-61248-151-7 (library binding : alk. paper) — ISBN 978-1-61248-152-4 (e-book)
    1. Musial, Stan, 1920-2013—Juvenile literature. 2. Baseball players—United States—
Biography—Juvenile literature. 3. St. Louis Cardinals (Baseball team)—History—Juvenile literature. I. Title.
    GV865.M8G343 2015
    796.357092–dc23
    [B]
                                                                    2015011357

Dedication
To Fran, in celebration of our fifty years of marriage.

The author thanks teachers Becky Sawyer and Ryan Glenn for their assistance in reviewing early drafts.

Contents

Introduction

Stan Musial first played baseball as a boy in a poor southwest Pennsylvania community in the early 1930s. He was blessed with enormous energy and talent. He could hit baseballs farther and pitch better than his classmates, but that wasn't good enough for Stan. He was determined to improve his skills. Stan was very competitive, but he was also very friendly and kind, and everyone liked him because of those qualities.

Stan's classmates and teachers knew he would be successful in life, but nobody anticipated the greatness he would achieve. He played with the St. Louis Cardinals for twenty-four years, during the time often described as the golden age of baseball. During that period the Redbirds won four National League championships. Stan retired in 1963 with a career batting average of .331 and 3,630 hits. Because of this, Stan Musial earned the distinction as one of the greatest hitters of all time.

Stan set batting records using a stance that was all his own. From a deep crouch, he twisted his body away from the plate in a cobra-like fashion and wiggled the bat and his hips as he waited for the pitch. Stan said he was crouching to make the strike zone smaller, but one coach had a better description. He said Stan "looks like a kid peeking around the corner to see if the cops are coming."

chapter 1

Donora, Pennsylvania

Stanislaus Francis Musial was born in Donora, Pennsylvania, on November 21, 1920, the fifth child and first son of Lukasz and Mary Musial. When he started school, his name was changed to Stanley Frank Musial. Donora was a hilly community of fourteen thousand people, located along the Monongahela River about twenty-one miles south of Pittsburgh.

Like many people in Donora, Stan's parents came from Eastern European countries. His father, Lukasz, was born in Poland and the parents of his mother, Mary, migrated from Austria-Hungary. Stan's parents and their families had come to the United States during the country's largest wave of immigration, which took place in the late 1800s and early 1900s.

Most of the men in Donora worked in factories of the American Steel and Wire Company, which was located on the banks of the Monongahela River. The factory provided good jobs for many people, but it also created a lot of pollution, and the pollution made Donora an unhealthy place to live. The smokestacks from the factory poured soot and dust from heavy metals into the air, along with carbon monoxide gas and sulfur fumes. Children playing outside got covered with black soot or yellowish residue and the dirty air was dangerous for people with asthma or other breathing problems.

Stash, or Stashu (a Polish nickname for Stanislaus), was nine years old when the Great Depression began

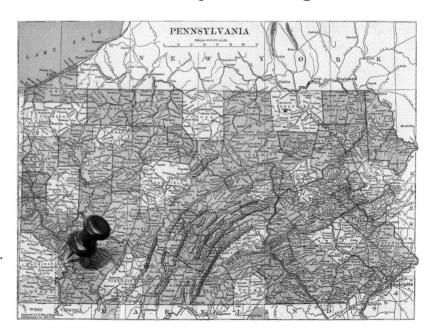

Many immigrants came to western Pennsylvania to work in the coal mines or in the factories and steel mills that grew up along the rivers in towns like Donora.

in fall 1929. During that nationwide financial crisis, the worst in the nation's history, many factories greatly reduced production or even shut down. Stan later recalled that his father worked only sometimes at the wire mill, and so his mother and four older sisters helped by doing domestic work. By 1932, the wire mill had temporarily shut down, and 90 percent of the workers in Donora were unemployed. Many in Donora survived only because they got food from charitable organizations. The Musials were among the very poor.

As a boy, Stan participated in gymnastics at the Polish Falcons Lodge in Donora, which helped him build up his muscles and develop his agility. His brother, Ed,

BIRD'S EYE VIEW, SHOWING AMERICAN STEEL & WIRE CO. WORKS, DONORA, PA.

The American Steel and Wire Company had a plant along the Monongahela River in Donora. Until the 1930s, many people worked twelve-hour shifts in factories like the ones in Donora.

The air pollution in Donora reached crisis levels in 1948 when weather conditions prevented the air from rising above the hills and cliffs around the town. A heavy smog covered the town for many days. About seven thousand people got sick from the smog. Six hundred people needed medical attention, and twenty died. Many people remained sick, and even after the smog lifted, another fifty people died. The story made national news.

recalled that Stan loved to compete in sports and fought to win at every turn. Stan played in summer baseball leagues, but he played other sports as well, including basketball.

In school, Stan was an average student. Like most of his classmates, he did not plan to go to college, so he took general classes in high school. He was especially good in wood shop. His shop teacher said that if Stan had not gone into baseball he would have been the world's best left-handed carpenter! Teachers described him as "the boy with the sunniest smile and [the] rosiest cheeks."

During a time when most schools were segregated, Donora had only one high school, where all students attended together. Stan played basketball and baseball with African-Americans students and, as usual, got along with everybody. One of Stan's teammates was Buddy Griffey, who played baseball. Buddy's grandson would be future Baseball Hall of Famer Ken Griffey Junior.

Stan was an outstanding basketball player at Donora High School, but he was an even better baseball player. He was a star left-handed pitcher and the team's best batter, hitting .455 as a high school senior. In both sports, he was assisted by two superior coaches: Ki Duda and Jimmie Russell.

Stan also played on teams in a regional league. His accomplishments on the baseball field meant that his name often appeared in the sports pages of local and regional newspapers. The favorable coverage attracted the attention of a scout for the St. Louis Cardinals, who later described his first impression.

> He had a pretty fair curve. I also liked the way he hit, but believe me, I had no idea that the skinny kid I saw that day would be the Stan Musial [of tomorrow]. He seemed to love to play ball, but he was very shy, almost the sort of kid you'd forget if you didn't look twice at the way he slugged the ball.

The scout from the Cardinals was not the only person Stan wanted to impress when he was in high school. During those years, Lillian Labash was very much a part of his life. Lil, as friends and family called her, was his high school sweetheart and the only girl he was ever serious about. Her father ran a grocery store near the downtown area and her family was of Russian heritage. Stan often walked to the Labash family's grocery store after school to visit Lil.

Stan did impress the scout and the Cardinals offered him a contract

The petite, attractive brown-haired Lil was known as "Shrimp" to her classmates. She was one year ahead of Stan in high school and had already graduated when Stan reported to the Cardinals' Class D team in June 1938.

Nicknames

to play for their Class D farm team, the equivalent of a rookie league today. Because Stan was only sixteen years old, his father had to agree and sign the contract to allow him to play. But Lukasz did not want his son to play professional baseball. Like most immigrant parents at that time, Lukasz wanted his son to finish high school and get a job at the local factory. There he would make more money than his starting salary of sixty-five dollars a month as a baseball player.

A journalist for a 1957 article in *Sport* magazine reported that Stan's father "was not anxious to have Stan sign up… thinking that Stan should go to work instead of wasting his time playing ball." Finally, Lukasz reluctantly signed the contract, agreeing that Stan would start playing professional baseball after he finished high school. ⚾

Chapter 2

On Rickey's Farm

Stan began his minor league career in Williamson, West Virginia, about 240 miles southwest of Donora. The Williamson Colts played in the Class D Mountain State League. The St. Louis Cardinals system had thirty-two teams and about five hundred minor league players. In Class D alone, there were twenty Cardinal affiliate teams. No other major league team managed a system that large, and Stan's chances of rising to the majors from a Class D team were slim.

Stan's first year was difficult. The team traveled by bus or in their own cars to play other teams in the league, often getting home in the early hours of the morning. In Williamson, there was little to do other than practice. Stan was so homesick that he questioned his decision to play professional baseball. He also struggled as a pitcher, having problems finding the strike zone. He finished the year with a 6–6 win-loss record while giving up more than four runs per game. And after being a local sports hero in Donora, he batted only .258 in his first year as a professional.

Stan's performance in the 1938 season meant he would return to Williamson for the 1939 season rather than moving up to a higher-level team.

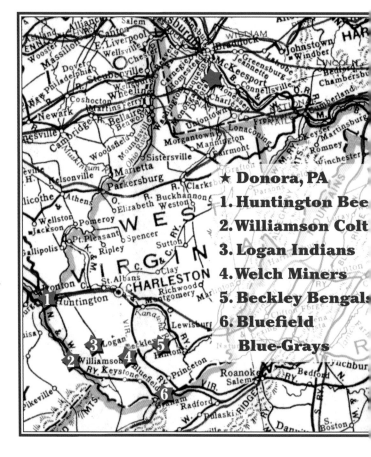

★ Donora, PA

1. Huntington Bee
2. Williamson Colt
3. Logan Indians
4. Welch Miners
5. Beckley Bengals
6. Bluefield Blue-Grays

The Mountain State League began play in 1937 with six teams located in towns in West Virginia. The Williamson team was originally called the Colts, but became the Red Birds in 1939. Stan Musial played for the Red Birds in 1939 and the team finished first in the league, but lost in the league finals to the Bluefield Blue-Grays.

That year, he showed some improvement, finishing with a 9–3 pitching record, an earned run average (ERA) of 4.30, and a batting average of .352. But the team manager was not optimistic.

> He will strike out just as many as he will walk, but I certainly can't depend on him, and most of the games he has won we have given him a dozen or more runs. . . I recommend his release because I don't believe he will ever be able to find the plate.

Fortunately, the Cardinals were not willing to give up on Stan, and he loved the game too much to give up on himself. Stan had another year to prove himself, but this meant one more year of Class D ball. Stan spent the 1940 season in Daytona Beach, playing for the Islanders in the Florida State League. Manager Dick Kerr, a former star pitcher for the Chicago White Sox, taught Stan how to better control his pitches and how to use his legs for more leverage on the mound. With Kerr's coaching, Stan turned into the league's best southpaw pitcher, with 18 wins and only 5 losses and a 2.62 ERA. While Stan was not pitching, he played outfield and batted .311. But what started as an outstanding season came to abrupt end on August 11 when Stan badly injured his left shoulder when diving to catch a ball. He would never again be able to pitch effectively.

Stan's (left) batting average in 1941 was .375, the highest in the Class C league. Coaching from Ollie Vanek (center), who was both a player and a manager for the team, helped Stan improve his hitting. Roy Broome (right) was also a batting star for the Springfield Cardinals.

While Stan was in Florida, he and Lil were married and their first child, a boy they named Dick, was born. During the off season, Stan sold sporting goods in a department store. He could have made more money by returning to Donora and getting a job at the factory, but Stan loved baseball too much to quit.

Stan went to minor league spring training in 1941 as damaged goods. The Cardinals organization was considering cutting him, but he showed promise as a hitter. So instead, the team assigned Stan to the Class C Springfield (Missouri) Cardinals.

Nobody expected how well Stan would perform that year. Ollie Vanek, who had originally signed Stan to a Cardinals contract, worked with Stan to strengthen his arm while playing him in right field. By May, Stan's batting average had reached .375, the highest in the league.

Stan continued to hit well, and on July 19, Cardinals general manager Branch Rickey went to White City Park to see him play. Rickey was impressed, and moved Stan up to the Double A Rochester (New York) Red Wings. Stan's final statistics for the Springfield Cardinals included a .379 batting average, 94 runs batted in, 100 runs scored, 27 doubles, 10 triples, 26 homers, and 15 stolen bases. He led his team in virtually every hitting category. The most surprising statistic was his 26 home runs. Never before had he displayed such power.

For the Rochester Red Wings, Stan played center field and continued to hit very well. He ended the

White City Park

The Springfield Cardinals played at White City Park, at the corner of Division and Boonville Avenues. It contained wooden grandstands on both sides of the infield and bleachers outside the left-field and right-field lines just beyond the infield. School kids could get in free by showing a pass given out by the Kiwanis organization or by returning a foul ball to the gatekeepers. White City Park was torn down after the 1942 season.

In his first game for the Rochester Red Wings, Stan hit a homer, a double, and two singles to help the Red Wings beat Baltimore 7–2. The team made it to the International League playoffs, where Stan's hitting helped them win two games before they were eliminated.

1941 season in mid-September with a batting average of .326. The team manager wrote a glowing report on Stan, and part of it appeared in the Rochester newspaper:

> The kid is an iceberg. If you tapped him you'd have to get ice water out of his veins. Yankee Stadium or a cow pasture—all parks are just another place to play ball to him.

After such a good season, Stan could look forward to returning to the Red Wings the next year. He returned to Donora expecting to spend time with his family now that his season was over. But much to Stan's surprise, he got a telegram telling him to report to the St. Louis Cardinals for their final twelve games. The Cardinals were in a pennant race with the Brooklyn Dodgers, but several key players had recently been injured. The team hoped Stan could help. Stan played his first game for the Cardinals on September 18, wearing number six. He was given that number because, of the uniforms available, that one fit him best. For the rest of his twenty-two seasons with the Cardinals, Stan Musial would never wear any other uniform number.

In that first game, a Sunday doubleheader against the Chicago Cubs, Stan had four consecutive hits, including two doubles and a stolen base in the first game and two hits in the second. He also made two great catches and threw out two runners at the plate. Billy Southworth, the Cardinals manager, cried out to one of his coaches, "That kid was born to play baseball." The Dodgers won the pennant, but in the remaining games of the season, Stan hit an amazing .426 with 20 hits in 47 at bats. He also performed outstandingly in the field and on the bases. But could Stan perform well over an entire season? ⚾

Chapter 3

Glory Years

The 1940s were wonderful years for Stan Musial and the Cardinals. Stan began to establish himself as a superstar, and the Cardinals emerged as the top team in the National League. Stan and his Cardinal teammates won four National League pennants and three World Series, and four second-place finishes were near misses.

In spring 1942, when Stan Musial moved to St. Louis to play for the Cardinals, the city was booming. The onset of World War II meant that companies that produced goods for the military were very busy. Plants were working at full capacity and many people were moving to St. Louis for jobs, including many blacks from the South.

But the city was still segregated. Blacks attended separate schools, many hotels and restaurants were off-limits, and Sportsman's Park, where the Cardinals played, was segregated until May 1944.

At first, Stan must have wondered whether there would even be a 1942 season, because the United States and her allies were at war with Germany, Italy, and Japan. When the season opened, some baseball players had already joined the military. During World War I, baseball had been suspended. But President Roosevelt had announced in January 1942, "I honestly feel that it would be best for the country to keep baseball going."

Major league baseball responded patriotically to the war effort. It became a regular ritual for "The Star

Over the years, the Cardinals logo has sometimes featured two birds on a bat and sometimes one bird. In the 1940s, the bat was black.

The Cardinals outfield in the early 1940s
featured Enos Slaughter, Terry Moore, and Stan Musial.
In the championship season of 1942, they were the National
League's best outfield. The next year, Moore and Slaughter
were in the military.

Spangled Banner" to be sung before each game, a practice
that continues today. Ball clubs encouraged players to
buy war bonds, which helped pay for the war, and teams
made donations to organizations that helped soldiers.

Stan started the 1942 season with a new contract
and a raise that made it possible for Lil and their son to
join him in St. Louis. Traveling around the country for
away games was difficult, and many players complained
about trying to sleep in crowded, noisy train cars and in
hotels without air conditioning. But Stan never seemed to

mind the inconveniences of the game. He had experienced much worse in his childhood in Donora.

Despite injuring his ankle early in the season, Stan played well in his rookie season. He and Johnny Beasley, another rookie, became the team's stars. Stan finished third in the league in team batting with a .315 average.

Stan called the Cardinals 1942 team, with its strong starting pitchers and team defense, the greatest team he ever played on. He said, "We felt like we were unbeatable… We had great spirit on that team." The Cardinals overcame their chief competitor, the Brooklyn Dodgers, late in the season and finished with 106 wins and only 48 losses. No National League team had won more since the Pittsburgh Pirates won 110 games in 1909. The Cardinals' winning season got them into the World Series, where they played the New York Yankees.

No one thought the Cardinals had much chance against the mighty Yankees, who had won eight World Series in eight attempts since 1927. The Yankees' star players, Joe DiMaggio, Charlie "King Kong" Keller, and Joe Gordon, had hit more home runs than any Cardinal, and they had pitchers as good as the Cardinals. The Yankees won the first game in the series, but Stan and the Cardinals won the next four, becoming the 1942 World Series champions.

The war had greater impact in the 1943 season. Two hundred major league baseball players were serving in the military, and they had been replaced by players brought up from farm teams. Traveling for away games was more difficult during wartime, with trains so crowded that players sometimes had to sit on their luggage because there were no seats available.

In the 1943 season, Stan won the batting title with a .357 average, the first of seven for him. He also led the league in hits (220), doubles (48), triples (20), and on-base percentage (.425). He won the National League Most

Stan took up playing the harmonica and often entertained his teammates when they traveled. Stan was shy, and playing the harmonica helped him connect to people. After he retired, he often played the harmonica at charity events and even recorded an album of harmonica music.

Valuable Player award, the first of three, and played in his first All-Star game, the first of many. What he could not do, however, was help win the World Series against the Yankees, who won it in five games.

By 1944, seven more Cardinal players had gone into the military, but the team still had enough talent to play in the World Series. Stan led the team with a batting average of .347, the second best in the National League, and the Cardinals beat the St. Louis Browns in six games.

After the 1944 season, it was finally Stan's turn to be called up for military service. Stan joined the U.S. Navy in January 1945 and served as a physical education instructor in Hawaii. Like so many other professional baseball players in the military, Stan spent much of his

Traveling as A Team

In the 1940s and 1950s, baseball teams usually traveled by train instead of by airplane. A typical road trip might last twenty-one days. The Cardinals would leave St. Louis Union Station after a Sunday doubleheader and head east. After the train crossed the Mississippi River, the players would eat in the dining car and then go to bed. When they woke up the next morning, they would be in Albany, New York. From there, they would head south along the scenic Hudson River to New York City. Train travel created strong bonds among players who spent so much time together.

SEPTEMBER 1948
20c

BASEBALL DIGEST

In this issue

STAN MUSIAL
DI MAGGIO
NEWHOUSER
RUSS MEYER

STAN MUSIAL
Cardinals

Stan finished the 1948 season leading the major leagues in batting average, hits, doubles, triples, total bases, and slugging percentage—and making the cover of *Baseball Digest* magazine.

time playing on a Navy baseball team to entertain the troops. During the war years, the best baseball teams anywhere were service teams.

Stan was accustomed to being away from home, but Hawaii was much farther away than he was used to. He missed Lil and their two children. But by September 1945, the war was over, and the 1946 season saw many baseball players returning to their teams.

Spring training was especially exciting that year. Returning players competed with replacement players for spots on the team. The baseball commissioner allowed teams to temporarily expand their rosters, and teams worked hard to get returning players back into condition for professional baseball.

Unlike some players, Stan came back from the war physically and mentally stronger than ever. He had one of his finest seasons in 1946, playing first base and carrying the ball club with his hitting. He led the league in virtually every batting category. He batted .365 with 228 hits, 124 runs scored, and with 50 doubles and 20 triples.

It was during the 1946 season that Stan got the nickname that would stick with him for the rest of his career. He peppered the short Dodgers' right field so often that fans there chanted "Here comes the man," hence Stan's new, long-lasting nickname, "Stan the Man."

The Cardinals faced the powerful Boston Red Sox in the World Series, which they won in seven games. Stan played a lesser role in that contest as others stepped up, including Enos Slaughter. His mad dash from first base on a hit to the outfield in the ninth inning secured the final game.

Stan began the 1947 season with various illnesses, which temporarily weakened him. As late as June 13, he was hitting only .202. For the rest of the season, he carried the team to a second-place finish in hitting .312. Stan was disappointed by his overall performance, but it was followed by the greatest season Stan ever had. In 1948, Stan batted .376 leading the major leagues in doubles (46) and triples (18). He led the National League in hits (230), and slammed 39 home runs, his most ever, while playing all three outfield positions and first base. In a game against the Boston Braves in September, Stan, playing with sprained wrists, had five hits while taking only five swings. In 1949, Stan again led the Cardinals with a .338 batting average with 36

Integration of Baseball

In 1947, Branch Rickey signed Jackie Robinson from the Negro Leagues to play for the Brooklyn Dodgers. Jackie was the first African-American to play major league baseball, but he was soon followed by future teammates and all-stars Roy Campanella and Don Newcombe. Jackie Robinson was inducted into the Baseball Hall of Fame in 1962.

homers as the team finished one game out of first place. The Cardinals again finished in second place, and the team's collapse soon followed.

In the mid-1940s, Cardinals owner Sam Breadon sold three key ballplayers to other teams, where they played very well against their old teammates. Also by that time, Branch

Stan loved the fans and was very gracious about signing autographs. He often chatted with fans, and especially enjoyed talking to children.

Rickey was working for the Dodgers, and the farm system he had set up for the Cardinals stopped producing good players. While Rickey began to recruit players from the Negro Leagues who contributed to the Dodgers' pennant-winning seasons, the Cardinals failed to follow suit and missed out on hiring some very good players. ⚾

Chapter 4

Player of the Decade

Stan remained one of the dominant superstars through the mid-1950s, winning four more National League batting titles (in 1950, 1951, 1952, and 1957). He finished near the top in hitting four more times and led the league in several other batting categories. He played, and often starred, in every All-Star game of the 1950s, and became the *Sporting News* Player of the Decade. Despite Stan's continued stardom, the Cardinals were never serious contenders for the World Series, except once. In 1957, they finished in second place.

These were bittersweet years for Stan. He added to his many individual honors, including reaching 3,000 hits in May 1958. He also set a National League mark by playing in 896 consecutive games. But Stan was often frustrated by the team's mediocre performance, as he struggled to keep the club in contention. He hid these disappointments very well, staying upbeat and playing hard at several positions. By now St. Louis had truly become home for Stan and Lil, and they enjoyed being involved in their children's activities.

Stan's kindness and cheerful behavior won the respect of his teammates, the fans, his opponents, and umpires. He reached out to struggling rookies and marginal players, often inviting them to join him for dinner or a show when they were on the road. As a star player, Stan often received samples from

In the Musial era, Topps and Bowman were the two largest baseball card companies.

31

Baseball Cards

Baseball card collecting has always been popular. It's a fun thing to do, and it's a good way to learn about the players. Collecting reached its peak in the 1980s. Some cards are very valuable, especially rookie cards and cards for Hall of Famers and baseball superstars. The value of the card depends on the popularity of the player, the condition of the card, and the number available. In 2010, a Topps rookie card of Mickey Mantle, in near-mint condition, sold for $130,000.

companies that wanted him to endorse their product. Stan shared those samples with rookie players, who earned much less money and were struggling financially. And no star player was more accommodating than Stan about autographs. He had only one rule after a ball game: let him get in his car and sit down before he started signing. Even when the temperature in St. Louis reached one hundred degrees, Stan would sit in his car and sign autographs, often chatting with fans for more than an hour.

Stan was friendly with players from opposing teams, even though team managers didn't want players to get friendly with the competition. He went out of his way to greet opposing players before the game or compliment them on recent accomplishments. Stan knew the names of most major leaguers, and also something about their

Stan formed lifelong friendships with many of his teammates. After Red Schoendienst (top picture, left) joined the Cardinals in 1945, he and Stan became close friends and often roomed together when the team was traveling. In the 1960s, Stan had been on the team for two decades, but he still made friends with newer Cardinals like George Altman (bottom picture, center) and Curt Flood (bottom picture, right).

backgrounds. One umpire wrote, "There was never a nicer fellow than Musial," a view that most umpires shared.

During one game, a couple of Stan's teammates taunted an African-American Dodger pitcher while he was on the pitching mound. The next evening, Stan went up to him to say, "I'm sorry that it happened, but don't let things like that bother

33

you. You're a good pitcher." Hall of Famer Henry Aaron, another African-American, said Stan was "one of my favorite ballplayers, because he treated everybody the same—black or white, superstar or scrub."

There was one day that stands out as extraordinary. On May 2, 1954, the Cardinals had a Sunday doubleheader in St. Louis against the New York Giants. Rain had cancelled batting practice that morning, and when the game started, Stan had a leg cramp. In the first inning, he limped to the plate and drew a walk. The fireworks began in the third inning when he hit a slow curve over the pavilion roof. He homered again to the right-field roof in the fifth on an inside fastball with a runner on base. He then singled on a curve ball in the sixth. Two innings later,

In 1953, ten-year-old Donna was attending a Cardinals game with her family. She said, "Stan Musial hit a ball into our seats— it actually grazed my knee." The next day, Stan autographed the ball for her. Donna recalled, "In those days the players parked across the ball park in the regular parking lot. There was little if any security. We always got to the game before the park opened and watched the players arrive. Mom got the autograph, she just stepped in front of him and asked him to sign and he did."

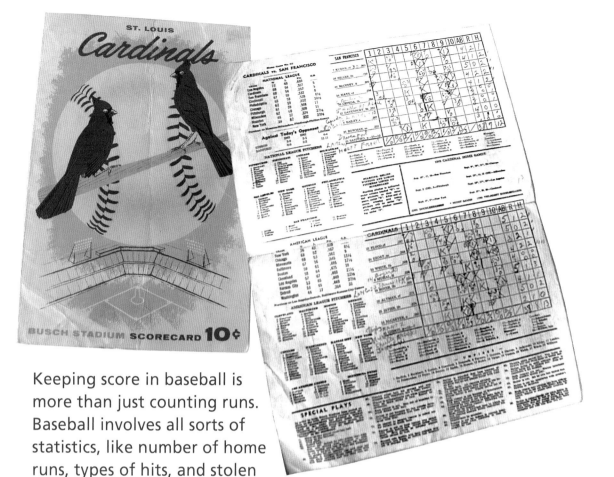

Keeping score in baseball is more than just counting runs. Baseball involves all sorts of statistics, like number of home runs, types of hits, and stolen bases. The most prominent for batters is batting averages. If a batter has 150 hits out of 400 official at bats (walks are not counted), you divide 150 by 400 for an average of .375. That is good enough to win the batting title!

with the score tied at six, he hammered a slider onto the right field roof. The Cardinals won 10 to 6.

Stan began the nightcap with a walk. In the third inning, he drove the ball 410 feet into deep right field where Willy Mays caught it in front of the bleachers, the longest ball Stan hit that day. He connected on a knuckler for his fourth homer in the fifth inning, and clubbed number five on a knuckler in the seventh. In his last plate appearance, an overeager Musial went after a bad pitch to pop up to the first baseman. The Cardinals lost 10 to 7, but Stan set a major league record of five home runs in a doubleheader that was unmatched until 1972. And his record of 21 total bases for a two-game set still stands.

By the late 1950s, Stan often found that he was feeling exhausted after games, especially after doubleheaders, and needed occasional games off. He also could no longer pull the outside pitch, his reflexes had slowed, and he had lost speed on the bases. He also became more vulnerable to leg injuries. By 1959, the thirty-eight-year-old Stan sensed that his career had entered its final years. He said that when he failed to hit .300, it would be time to retire.

During the 1959 season, Stan hit .255, his worst major league season ever, but he refused to retire. Stan felt he could still help the club and he still had some career goals to achieve. Most importantly, there was nothing he would rather do than play baseball. After the season ended, he underwent a rigorous conditioning program to prepare him for the 1960 season. Despite all his work, he was hitting only .268 on May 7, and he was benched for a while. After Stan returned to the lineup, he was hitting better, and finished the season with a .275 average. He finished the 1961 season hitting .288, with 15 home runs.

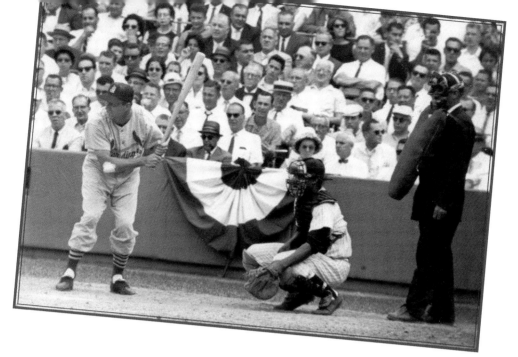

After two poor seasons, no one expected Stan to play well in 1962. But manager Johnny Keane still saw Stan as a major asset. At the age of forty-two, Stan managed to hit .330, the third highest average in the National League. Nobody his age had ever hit that well. In the process, he broke a number of career hit records, including Honus Wagner's National League career record of 3,430 hits. After these successes, Stan decided to play one more season. But in 1963, Stan had problems with nagging injuries and long slumps, and he finished with only a .255 average.

Stan played his final game for the Cardinals on Sunday, September 29, 1963, against the Cincinnati Reds. The pregame ceremonies were something to behold, with TV cameras and photographers there to see sports officials praise Stan Musial. Baseball Commissioner Ford Frick said, "Here stands baseball's perfect warrior. Here stands baseball's perfect knight."

After thanking his family and others for their support and God for giving him the talent and good health to play baseball, Stan barely managed to finish his speech with these words: "I hate to say good-bye. So until we meet again, I want to thank you very much." Stan wiped his eyes and kissed Lil, then they climbed into an open convertible and were driven slowly around the park.

During his last game, Stan did not disappoint. He singled twice, the last being his 3,630th hit. Afterward, Stan said, "You know, that's the way I came in. Two base hits. And that's the way I leave."

Stan retired from the Cardinals team in 1963, but he never stopped being a Cardinal. He remained part of the Cardinals family and participated in opening-day ceremonies every year until his death. In 2009, sportscaster Bob Costas looked back at Stan's career and commented, "Musial represents ... more than two decades of sustained excellence and complete decency as a human being."

Chapter 5

Staying Active

Many ballplayers, after years in the limelight, find retirement difficult, either because of financial reasons or because they no longer feel important. Not Stan. He remained active and in demand during his retirement years. Stan had always advised players to prepare for retirement by looking for other ways to earn money.

He took his own advice when he partnered with Jules "Biggie" Garagnani to open a restaurant in St. Louis. Stan Musial's and Biggie's, as it was called, was very successful well into the 1970s. Stan and Biggie also invested in real estate, including a bowling alley in St. Louis and a hotel in Florida.

Stan Musial served on the President's Council on Physical Fitness from 1964 to 1967. The Council encourages lifetime fitness by participating in sport and active games. The Council also gives the Physical Fitness Award for achievements by boys and girls from ten to seventeen years old.

Immediately after retiring, Stan became a Cardinal vice president and served as advisor to President Lyndon Johnson on physical fitness. He also published his autobiography, titled *Stan Musial: "The Man's" Own Story*.

In 1966, Stan, along with Hank Aaron of the Atlanta Braves, Brooks Robinson of the Baltimore Orioles, and other baseball personalities, traveled to Vietnam to entertain American soldiers serving there. The group visited camps, hospitals, and air bases to sign autographs, shake hands, and show films of the All-Star game.

In 1967, Stan became the Cardinals general manager. He was one of only three former players to serve in that capacity. He soon improved player morale and relations with the press. That year, the Cardinals won the pennant and the World Series.

Two years later, Stan was inducted into the Baseball Hall of Fame. He called that honor his "greatest baseball thrill" ever. He was soon asked to serve on the Hall of Fame's veterans' committee, which evaluated for induction players who had been previously passed over.

For many years Stan acted as the unofficial ambassador of baseball. His sunny, warm, and caring personality enlivened many charitable events. Stan and Lil also visited Poland, the birthplace of Stan's father. On their first trip to Poland, in the early 1970s, Stan and Lil delivered official letters from Cardinal Carberry of St. Louis to the cardinals in Warsaw and Krakow. The cardinal of Krakow was a friend

MUSIAL

A Statue of Stan

Stan Musial was known for his love of children. When it was decided to put up a statue of him in front of Busch Stadium, he wanted it to portray a boy gazing upward as Stan, with a baseball bat leaning against his hip, signed an autograph. Instead, the mayor of St. Louis commissioned a sculptor who featured Stan in a batting stance that bore little resemblance to Musial's. That statue still exists at Busch Stadium.

of Cardinal Carberry's, and he later became Pope John Paul II. On that trip, Stan presented a baseball to the cardinal of Krakow. He signed it, "To Cardinal Wojtyla from Cardinal Musial."

In 1990, Stan and Lil traveled to Poland with Philadelphia donor Edward Piszek and his wife. They carried a gift of 486 bats, 250 gloves, and 925 Cardinals baseball caps that enabled the city of Wroclaw to start a Little League baseball program. Stan's efforts to establish baseball as a youth sport in Poland were successful, and Little League baseball soon involved more than three thousand children on thirty teams in six Polish cities. Among Polish children, Stan Musial remains a hero.

As Stan got older, he had various health problems that made it more difficult for him to remain active. In 1983 he overcame prostate cancer, but old baseball injuries caused him to limp, and he appeared frail when he reached his seventies. When he was in his mid-eighties, Stan was diagnosed with Alzheimer's disease, which severely weakened him.

President Barack Obama awarded Stan Musial the Presidential Medal of Freedom on February 15, 2011. The president paid Stan the ultimate compliment when he said, "Stan remains, to this day, an icon untarnished; a beloved pillar of the community; a gentleman you'd want your kids to emulate."

Stan died quietly at his home on January 19, 2013, at the age of ninety-two. Baseball Commissioner Bud Selig said, "He was the heart and soul of the historic Cardinals franchise for generations. . . . Stan's life embodies baseball's unparalleled history and why this game is the national pastime."

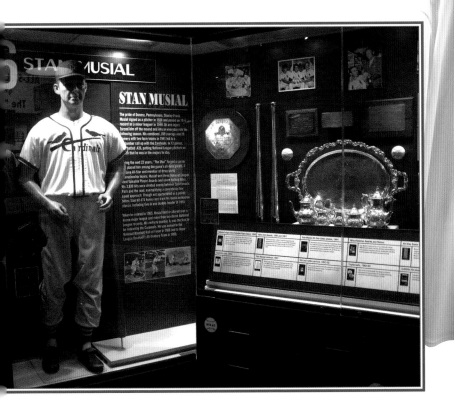

Stan the Man

Stan Musial was raised in a poor community in the midst of the Great Depression, but he became one of America's greatest baseball players ever. Stan had a lot of natural talent, but he was also a hard worker who always tried to improve his performance. He is known and respected for his many baseball records and honors. The records he set may be broken, but nobody will ever forget his devotion to baseball and his endless good spirits.

Stan was probably the first player to be friendly with opposing players during games, a common practice with present-day players. He encouraged players to plan for the future by saving their money and finding other occupations to pursue after they retired. Stan loved and cared about people, especially children. He was known for his modesty, his acts of kindness, his cheerfulness, and his desire to make people happy. He was devoted to his family, to his community, and to his team, the St. Louis Cardinals.

For all these reasons, Stan Musial was not merely a celebrity who was well-known and worshiped by fans. He was a true hero. It is with good reason that Stan Musial is still known affectionately as "Stan the Man."

Timeline

November 21, 1920: Stan Musial was born in Donora, Pennsylvania.

1929: The Great Depression began; many workers lost their jobs when factories closed.

1936: As a teenager, Stan played baseball in a regional league.

1937: Stan signed a contract with the St. Louis Cardinals.

1938: Stan starred in baseball and basketball for Donora High School.

1938–1939: Stan played for the Class D Williamson Colts/Red Birds.

1940: Stan played for the Daytona Beach (Florida) Islanders. In May, Stan and Lil were married. Their son Richard (Dick) was born.

1941: Stan played for the Springfield Cardinals, then the Rochester Red Wings. On September 17, Stan played his first game with the St. Louis Cardinals.

1942: Cardinals won the World Series, with Stan playing a key role.

1943: On July 13, Stan appeared in his first annual All-Star game. He would appear in twenty-five All-Star games during his career.

1944: Stan and Lil's daughter Gerry was born in December.

1945–1946: Stan joined the Navy in January 1945 and was discharged in March 1946.

1946: Stan won the batting title with a .365 average. The Cardinals won the World Series.

1948: Stan had his best all-time season as he hit .376, the highest average in the major leagues.

1950: Stan and Lil's daughter Janet was born.

1956: *Sporting News* named Stan Player of the Decade for the 1946 to 1955 era.

1958: Stan and Lil's daughter Jean was born.

1962: After several poor seasons, Stan hit .330, the highest average a forty-two-year-old had ever achieved in the major leagues in the twentieth century.

September 29, 1963: Stan played his final game in the major leagues.

1967: As Cardinals general manager, Stan led the team to a World Series championship.

1969: Stan was inducted into the Baseball Hall of Fame in his first year of eligibility.

February 15, 2011: Stan was awarded the Presidential Medal of Freedom by President Barack Obama.

January 19, 2013: Stan died at the age of ninety-two.

For Further Reading

For Young Readers

Cline-Ransome, Lesa. *Satchel Paige*. New York: Simon and Schuster, 2000.

Glaser, Jason. *Jackie Robinson: Baseball's Great Pioneer*. North Mankato, MN: Graphic Library, 2006.

Grey, Vivian. *Moe Berg: The Spy Behind Home Plate*. Philadelphia: JPS Publication Society, 1996.

Hampton, William. *Babe Ruth (Up Close)*. New York: Viking Juvenile, 2009.

Hurwitz, Joanna. *Baseball Fever*. New York: Harper Collins, 2000.

Kellogg, David. *True Stories of Baseball's Hall of Famers*. San Mateo, CA: Bluewood Books, 2000.

Pellowski, Michael J. *The Chicago Black Sox Baseball Scandal: A Headline Court Case*. Berkeley, NJ: Enslow Publishers, 2003.

Sommer, Shelley. *Hammerin' Hank Greenberg: Baseball Pioneer*. Honesdale, PA: Boyds Mills Press, 2011.

Websites

Donora Historical Society and Smog Museum. *1948 Smog*. https://sites.google.com/site/donorahistoricalsociety/1948-smog.

Donora Historical Society. *Stan the Man Musial*. https://sites.google.com/site/donorahistoricalsociety/stan-musial.

Finkel, Jan. *Stan Musial*. Society for American Baseball Research. http://sabr.org/bioproj/person/2142e2e5.

How to Keep Score in Baseball: How to Use a Baseball Score-card. https://www.youtube.com/watch?v=03FHoHZl4os.

National Baseball Hall of Fame. baseball.org.

St. Louis Cardinals. *Stan Musial, 1920–2013.* http://stlouis.car-dinals.mlb.com/stl/fan_forum/stan_musial.jsp?loc=bio.

Universal International News (newsreel). *1962 All Star Game* (excerpts). https://www.youtube.com/watch?x-yt-ts=1422579428&x-yt-cl=85114404&v=0_1csSHxcvs.

ESPN. *Sports Century: Stan Musial.* ESPN documentary, 2001. Available online at https://www.youtube.com/watch?v=LIJI1Lid5tU

Sources

Giglio, James N. *Musial: From Stash to Stan the Man.* Columbia: University of Missouri Press, 2007.

———. "Prelude to Greatness: Stanley Musial and the Spring-field Cardinals of 1941." *Missouri Historical Review* 90 (July 1996): 429–52.

Goldstein, Richard. *Spartan Seasons: How Baseball Survived the Second World War.* New York: Macmillan, 1980.

Hoffer, Richard. "Stan Musial, 1920–2013." *Sports Illustrated*, January 28, 2013.

Marshall, William. *Baseball's Pivotal Era: 1945–1951.* Lexing-ton: University of Kentucky Press, 1999.

Rains, Rob. *The St. Louis Cardinals: The 100th Anniversary His-tory.* New York: St. Martin's Press, 1992.

Turner, Frederick. *When the Boys Came Back: Baseball and 1946.* New York: Henry Holt, 1996.

Vecsey, George. *Stan Musial: An American Life.* New York: Bal-lantine Books, 2012.

Index

Image Credits

Original art by John Hare: pgs. 6, 13, 20, 30, and 39.

Courtesy of National Baseball Hall of Fame and Museum: cover, Stan Musial running bases, 1942; p. 4, Stan Musial in Cardinals uniform, 1942; p. 18, Stan Musial and Gene Pillard, Rochester Red Wings, 1941; p. 33 (top), Stan Musial and Red Schoendienst, 1940s; p. 33 (bottom), Stan Musial, George Altman, and Curt Flood, 1963; p. 37, Stan Musial at bat.

United States Digital Map Library, US GenWeb Archives Project: p. 7, detail of *Map of Pennsylvania* (New York: C. S. Hammond & Co. Atlas, 1910).

Courtesy of Donora Historical Society: p. 8, Bird's-Eye view, showing American Steel & Wire Co. Works, Donora, PA, ca. 1910; p. 10, Stan Musial high school basketball team, 1938; p. 11, Lillian Labash's Donora High School Yearbook photo, 1938.

Library of Congress, Prints and Photographs Division: p. 9, The wire mill, Donora, PA, ca. 1910 (LC-USZ62-131258); p. 14, detail of *Map of Principal Transportation Lines of the United States* (New York: Rand McNally, 1921); p. 28, Jackie Robinson of the Brooklyn Dodgers, 1954, *Look Magazine* Photograph Collection (LC-L9-54-3566-0).

Courtesy of *Springfield News-Leader*: p. 16, Stan Musial, Ollie Vanek, and Roy Broome, Springfield Cardinals, 1941.

Courtesy of Cardinals Hall of Fame and Museum: p. 21, cardinals logo, 1940s; p. 24, harmonica and Stan Musial harmonica book; p. 41, Stan Musial statue; p. 43, Stan Musial display (photos by Barbara Smith-Mandell).

Courtesy of *Sporting News*: p. 22, Enos Slaughter, Terry Moore, and Stan Musial, St. Louis Cardinals, early 1940s; p. 29, Stan Musial signing an autograph for a young fan, 1943; p. 38, Stan Musial's farewell speech, September 29, 1963.

Courtesy of *Baseball Digest*: p. 26, cover of September 1948 *Baseball Digest* magazine.

Private collection of Mandell family: pgs. 26–27, Louisville Slugger bats (photo by Lisa Ahrens).

Courtesy of The Topps Company, Inc.: p. 31 (top), Topps® baseball card, 1958 All Star #376 Stan Musial.

Courtesy of Upper Deck: p. 31 (middle and bottom), commemorative cards, 1999: St. Louis Cardinals, Stan Musial (NC1); Stan Musial, Monumental Moments, Life in Donora (NC2).

Private collection of Don and Margaret Duke: p. 34, baseball autographed by Stan Musial; p. 35, Cardinals scorecards, 1950s (photos by Lisa Ahrens).

Private collection of Chris Jewett: p. 43, Stan Musial souvenir shirt (photo by Lisa Ahrens).

iStock photo.com: p. 40, Children on climbing wall (#35330386).

Thank you to the Missouri Humanities Council for funding assistance in licensing images for this book.